A Hiccup Cake

Story by Janie Spaht Gill, Ph.D.
Illustrations by Bob Reese

DOMINIE PRESS

Pearson Learning Group

"I have the hiccups, Mom. What's up?

2

Hiccup! Hiccup! Hiccup!"

4

"Stand on your head
and count to ten."

Bobby did, and then...

"Hiccup!

Hiccup!

Hiccup!"

"Rub your stomach, scratch your head, and count to ten."

Bobby did, and then...

"Hiccup!
Hiccup!
Hiccup!"

11

"Go and hide and count to ten."

Bobby did, and then...

"Hiccup! Hiccup! Hiccup!"

14

"Boo! I scared you!
I scared away
your hiccups, too."

"Yea! Yea!
My hiccups have
all gone away!"

"Let's celebrate and bake a cake! What kind of cake should we bake?"

"How about a hiccup cake?"

"Hiccup! Hiccup! Hiccup!"

21

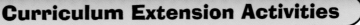

A Hiccup Cake

- Take this opportunity to help the children develop oral language by having them recall the last time they had the hiccups and how they got rid of them. Encourage them to write letters to the boy in the story, giving him other popular suggestions for getting rid of hiccups. For example, hopping on one foot or doing summersaults. Have the children illustrate their letters.

- Brainstorm a list of cakes of different flavors and write them on the board. Then have the children draw a picture of their favorite type of cake on a sheet of paper. Across the bottom of a chart, write the different flavors of cakes the children named. Then have them cut out and glue their favorite cake in the appropriate column, thereby creating a bar graph. Which cake was the most popular? Which was the least popular?

- Play a sound game in which the children close their eyes while one child makes a sound (hiccups, coughing, sneezing, sniffing, giggling, etc.). Then have the children guess the sound.

About the Author

Dr. Janie Spaht Gill brings twenty-five years of teaching experience to her books for young children. During her career thus far, she has taught at every grade level, from kindergarten through college. Gill has a Ph.D. in reading education, with a minor in creative writing. She is currently residing in Lafayette, Louisiana with her husband, Richard. Her fresh, humorous topics are inspired by the things her students say in the classroom. Gill was voted the 1999-2000 Louisiana Elementary Teacher of the Year for her outstanding work in primary education.

Softcover Edition ISBN 0-7685-2162-9
Library Bound Edition ISBN 0-7685-2470-9

Printed in Singapore
4 5 6 7 8 9 10   10 09 08 07

1-800-321-3106
www.pearsonlearning.com